DUCKS & WATERFOWL

A PORTRAIT OF THE ANIMAL WORLD

MARCUS SCHNECK

TODTRI

This book was designed and produced by
TODTRI Book Publishers
P.O. Box 572, New York, NY 10116-0572
FAX: (212) 695-6984
e-mail: info@todtri.com

Printed and bound in Singapore

ISBN 1-57717-131-4

Author: Marcus Schneck

Publisher: Robert M. Tod
Senior Editor: Edward Douglas
Book Designer: Mark Weinberg
Typesetting: Command-O, NYC

Visit us on the web!
www.todtri.com

PHOTO CREDITS
Photo Source/Page Number

Theo Allofs, 23, 62 (bottom), 63 (bottom), 65 (top)

Peter Arnold, Inc.
Steven Fuller, 68 (bottom)
Klein-Hubert, 60
Stephen J. Krasemann, 62 (top)
Thomas D. Mangelsen, 53, 66, 60 (bottom), 70
Carl R. Sams, 15, 56–57
Roland Seitre, 67
Günther Ziesler, 71

Joe McDonald, 21, 28, 31, 44, 49 (top)

Picture Perfect
Peter Adams/Ace, 40–41
Steve Bentsen, 17, 22, 59 (top)
N. R. Christensen, 4, 10, 20 (top & bottom), 39 (bottom), 49 (bottom)
William B. Folsom, 32 (bottom), 36
Imagery/Scott Nielsen, 6, 8–9, 11 (top), 13, 14, 18, 24–25, 27 (top & bottom),
29, 30 (top & bottom), 37, 38, 47, 48, 54 (bottom), 63 (top)
Ann Jacobi, 16
Warren Jacobi, 34, 68 (top)
Stephen Kirkpatrick, 7, 39 (top), 50–51
Maryelle McGrath, 65 (botom)
The Martin Library, 11 (bottom), 12
Wayne Shields, 43
Paul Sterry, 33, 61
John W. Warden, 3, 5, 19 (right), 26, 32 (top), 35 (top & bottom), 42, 45,
46 (top & bottom), 52, 54 (top), 55 (top & bottom), 58, 59 (bottom)
David F. Wisse, 64, 69 (top)

INTRODUCTION

The migrations of geese and other water-fowl have been harbingers of the changing seasons for people throughout history.

The hunter cupped a hand to his forehead, shielding his eyes from the bright sun. He gazed in awe as geese beyond his counting passed overhead, following the great river north on the early spring leg of their annual migration. The string of his bow seemed to bite into the skin of his shoulder, urging for the chance to lose an arrow at such abundance of game. The mindless weapon could not know that no shaft could reach far enough into the heavens to bring down one of the great birds. But the warrior knew this was not an opportunity for meat for the lodge. Instead he stood on the bank of the river, above the churning waters of some rapids, and opened his ears to gather in the siren call of the geese. His heart jumped with the coming of another spring.

Not far away, two travelers tilted back their heads, raising their separate sets of binoculars to their eyes. They gazed in awe as geese beyond counting filled the lenses of their instruments, coursing northward along the great river that generations of geese had followed. The cameras in the car seemed to call for their use, urging for the chance to capture this spectacle of nature. But the watchers accepted the moment for one of reflection rather than recording. They simply stood on the bank of the river, hearing the churning water of the rapids mix with the honking of the geese and savoring the coming of another spring.

Waterfowl—ducks and geese, primarily—have long held the power to inspire in humans a reverence for things wild and massive. Their great numbers, their movement on a grand scale, and their response to the clock of nature appeal to us all. Generations have marked the change of season by the passing of the flocks.

THE NATURE OF WATERFOWL

The fossil record suggests that the family Anatidae (ducks, geese, and swans) in the order Anseriformes extends back more than 80 million years, into the late Mesozoic era, which is commonly referred to as the Age of the Dinosaurs. Actually, fossil Anatidae date into the Campanian age, which occurred in the late Cretaceous period, which came towards the end of the Mesozoic Era. It was a period that the fossil record has shown to be the final flowering of the dinosaurs, with groups like the pachycephalosaurs, hadrosaurs, and tyrannosaurs arising. It also saw the first great diversification of birds, which are commonly viewed as living dinosaurs today.

Anatomy

Although the 150 or so species that make up the Family Anatidae (waterfowl) appear quite distinct from one another on the surface, most are very much alike in form and function. All have relatively large bodies, topped by relatively long necks. With few exceptions, notably the fish-hunters, all waterfowl species have short, straight bills. All have rather short

Although mallards in city parks are more often seen waddling after the next hand-out of bread crumbs, the species often feeds by up-ending as they swim.

Geese appear much larger than they actually are, covered by heavy feathers over a thick layer of insulating down.

legs set far back on the body, ending in webbed feet. These are wonderful means of propulsion, on and in the water, but make the birds somewhat awkward on land. All have outer feathers tightly layered and kept waterproof by the bird's regular application of oil from a gland near its tail, over a thick layer of soft, insulating down.

After the breeding season, waterfowl molt to replace the worn feathers of the previous years with new. During the molt, the birds are unable to fly, because all of the wing feathers are lost at the same time. This is not the case with most other families of birds, which tend to lose just one feather at a time from each wing.

Migration

Most waterfowl are gregarious birds, as is evident in the large flocks they form during the spring and fall migrations. The concept of migration and the image of certain waterfowl species, notably geese flying in a huge "V" formation overhead, are etched in the human memory. Many ducks, pelicans, and cranes use the same aerodynamic flight pattern in their migrating flocks, but it is the migration of geese that man has long considered to be the harbinger of spring and winter.

Migration, simply defined, is the seasonal movement of animals from one region to another in search of abundant food and fair

weather. Birds are not alone in such movements. Many animals from eels and salmon to reindeer and zebra migrate. But birds, notably some waterfowl species, have become the poster species for migration.

In migration, waterfowl generally follow well-defined, time-honored paths, marked by valleys and mountain ridges, coasts, and rivers. Barring unusual weather interference, migrating geese today pretty much follow the same routes their predecessors have followed for thousands of years.

Some bird species migrate in sexually distinct patterns. Either males or females leave first, followed several days, or weeks, later by the other sex. Geese, that mate for life, however, migrate with their mates, joining in large flocks for the trip.

Migrating birds are capable of considerable speeds while on the move. Some duck species, for example, have been clocked at nearly 60 miles (96 kilometers) per hour. They could complete their entire trip in a very short time but at great costs to their health and reserves. Instead, most species fly for much of a day and then pause for a few days of rest and feeding. Some songbirds and shorebirds migrate through the nighttime hours and then stop to feed by day, but waterfowl are generally daytime migrants.

Most migrate at relatively low altitudes, low enough for their plaintiff honking or other calls to be heard on the ground. In northwestern India, however, migrating flocks of geese have been recorded at altitudes of nearly 30,000 feet (9,140 meters) above sea level.

Although the relatively large and bulky body of this canvasback causes it to patter across the surface of the water before taking off, once aloft it is a fast, strong flyer.

FOLLOWING PAGE: A small flock of ducks prepares for their morning feeding as the sun rises over the marsh.

Like many African species, the Cape teal is an opportunistic breeder, moving into lowlands whenever seasonal flooding provides sufficient water.

True migration generally takes place around the same time every year, with the same birds generally migrating to the same destinations. Nomadic flights to take advantage of quickly changing environmental conditions are a behavior similar to migration, but generally of shorter duration, with destinations that are not so fixed historically. For instance, in the arid regions of Australia and Africa, when rains do come, ducks and other species quickly congregate to breed at the bodies of water that form from the long-awaited downpour.

Successful navigation over long migration routes is the result of many factors. Landmarks, such as mountains, rivers, and coasts, play a part. Birds also can see the ultraviolet light rays of the sun and can hear very low-frequency sounds, such as wind colliding with the sides of mountains, over long distances. They also seem endowed with a sense of direction that allows them to fly in a constant path. The Earth's magnetic fields also provide important clues to birds on the move, probably through the angle between the lines of the magnetic fields and the planet's horizontal plane rather than the polarity of the fields.

Migratory birds build up fat reserves in the tissues of their body in the period leading up to the start of their migratory flights, responding to metabolic changes triggered by hormones secreted by their pituitary gland, which is located at the base of the brain. But the actual beginning of the flight is more likely triggered by environmental changes, such as a growing scarcity of food or sudden weather changes.

The common merganser is a migratory species, as are most ducks, but it tends to remain close to its summer breeding grounds as long into the winter as there are areas of water that remain free of ice.

Flocks of bar-headed geese regularly migrate over the Himalayan Mountains in their seasonal passage from central Asia to northern India.

Nesting

At the end of the spring migration, mating occurs and soon a new generation is born and raised in carefully constructed nests. Waterfowl nests generally are made on the ground near water. For many species, they are simple depressions that the birds line with plant fibers and down they pluck from their own bodies. Some species, such as the wood duck, make their nests in tree cavities. And, a few species have been known to choose quite unusual spots for their nests. In areas where it is not heavily hunted, the ruddy shelduck, for example, sometimes lays its eggs in buildings. Hatchling waterfowl are mostly precocious, able to find their own food immediately upon emerging from the egg.

A freshly hatched pintail chick lies exhausted among the eggs of its future brothers and sisters, while another of the brood begins the hole in its shell that will be expanded to gain freedom.

DUCKS

Few regions of the world, outside the arid desert regions and ice-locked Antarctica, are without some representatives of the group of life known as ducks. Some species, like the mallard, ranging across nearly all of the northern hemisphere, are incredibly widespread. Others, like the pink-headed duck of northeastern India, are as rare as the mallard is common, and perhaps may even be extinct. However, with the long-distance migrations of many ducks, some species can generally be found just about everywhere on the planet.

In many species of duck the male, or drake, carries more colorful and showy outer feathers than the female, or hen, particularly during the breeding season. Immature birds, in those species that show a marked sexual difference, also are generally more subdued in appearance than adult drakes. Both sexes of some species also display a wing patch of bright colors, known as the speculum.

Many species of duck have been domesticated. They are raised commercially as food and for their eggs and down. In domestication, ducks are a very hardy group of fowl. They require only the most basic housing and pen conditions. Many don't even need water to swim in, although all will take advantage of any that is provided. They also are relatively free of parasites and disease.

Like most bird species, ducks regularly take advantage of opportunities to bathe, which may come more regularly to waterfowl species.

Some of the brightest colors in the animal kingdom are displayed among the males, or drakes, of many duck species. The drake mallard is among the most readily identifable of waterfowl.

Whistling Ducks

Scientists study ducks and classify them in several different ways, but one of the most common is by their habits and by what they eat. The aptly named whistling ducks are a widespread group with a shrill whistle of a call. They are very vocal birds, both on the ground, in water, and in flight. A flock of lesser whistling ducks, for example, maintains a near constant rattle as they alight or land.

They once were known as tree ducks for their occasional nesting in trees, however that is not a universal habit among any of the species and, instead, occurs in some populations while not in others, or under certain circumstances. The fulvous whistling duck, for example, places its nest among the low vegetation at the edge of bodies of freshwater in the southern United States but is said to be primarily a tree-nester in India. In contrast, the black-bellied whistling duck is an accomplished grazer and much less restricted to the water than many of its fellows.

Whistling ducks are generally shy and wary. When alarmed they respond much the same as geese, raising their heads to scan all around them. Except when they are seen in flight, they often are first observed as a group of heads jutting from the vegetation. They are gregarious with their own and other species, and are generally found in small flocks. Sexes are similar in appearance.

The flight of whistling ducks is strong, propelled by relatively slow wingbeats. The feet project behind the tail, with both head and feet below the line of the body. To land, whistling ducks extend their head and feet downward until the bill almost comes into contact with the ground.

Whistling ducks generally feed at night in shallow freshwater lakes and ponds with abundant vegetation along the shoreline. Rice fields are favored feeding sites in some locales. They spend most of their time in the water, dabbling. Flocks regularly are seen diving in unison. They will feed on land, but never far from water.

The fulvous whistling duck is widely distributed over the Americas, Africa, and the Indian subcontinent, although localized in its occurrence. The lesser whistling duck occurs as a year-round resident across much of its range, which extends throughout most of tropical Asia. The white-faced whistling duck is widespread across southeastern Africa and Central and South America, although in a spotty pattern throughout its range. The black-bellied whistling duck is widespread across the southern United States, Central America, and South America, sometimes abundant locally.

Male colors, such as the bright red bill of the shelduck, generally are more brilliant among waterfowl during the breeding season than at other times of the year.

Shelducks

Shelducks and shelgeese of the subfamily Tadorninae are in many ways an intermediate group between true ducks and true geese. In feeding habits, all members of the subfamily are nearly as terrestrial as they are aquatic, and some could almost be described as land-based.

Like most species in this subfamily, the spur-winged goose of tropical Africa is generally a shy and wary creature, but it will put up a strong defense of its nest, bringing the spurs at the bends of its wings into place.

The comb duck is closest to shelducks in evolutionary development and generally considered with the subfamily, although it is a highly unique species often placed in a tribe of its own, Sarkidiornini. Another common name, knob-billed goose, is most descriptive of the large fleshy knob near the base of the male's bill. In two distinct races, the comb duck is spread across tropical Africa and Asia, and South America.

Although males gather small harems of females on the breeding grounds, comb ducks are generally sociable birds that can be found in loose colonies even on the breeding grounds.

The shelduck is among the most attractive water-fowl species native to Europe, known for its large molt gatherings off the northern coast of Germany.

The ruddy duck, alone here, is most commonly encountered in large rafts of birds outside the breeding season.

Habitat loss has decimated many waterfowl populations around the globe, including that of the ruddy shelduck in Europe, where the species is now quite rare.

The ruddy shelduck may gather by the thousands on favored wintering grounds or during the molt, but it is more commonly spotted in small parties or pairs throughout its range in northwestern Africa, Europe, and Asia. In many parts of its range it is a very shy and wary bird, but in other areas it has become very accepting of human presence, even to the point of nesting inside buildings. The nests are often placed far from water, in burrows, tree cavities, and even buildings.

The multi-colored shelduck, generally considered one of the most beautiful of European waterfowl, is noted for gathering in congregations as large as 100,000 birds along Germany's northern coast during the molt.

Torrent ducks are at ease in the rushing streams of the Andes Mountains, winding their way up waterfalls and through rapids.

When feeding they move through the water completely submerged, clambering out onto rocks to rest from time to time.

Related to the shelducks are the large, stocky steamer ducks of the coasts of South America. Their name "steamer" is derived from their habit of paddling feverishly to splash across the surface of the water when being pursued. Most species in this genus are incapable of anything more than short, clumsy flights. They prefer to "steam" across the water when threatened, taking the air as a last resort.

The flying steamer duck is the one exception, although its strong flight ability is generally reserved for the pre-breeding period when moving inland to find nesting sites. In addition, many individuals and some populations of even the flying steamer duck are flightless throughout the year.

Some duck species, while common within their range, are extremely limited geographically. The Magellanic flightless steamer duck, for example, occurs only along the coasts of Chile and southern Argentina.

Dabbling Ducks

Dabbling ducks, the largest group, are thus named for their habit of upending in the water, with their head underwater and their tail and feet in the air, to explore the bottom of a pond with their bills, searching for insect larvae, shellfish, and other small creatures to eat. Many of this group also feed at the surface, eating plant and insect life they find there. They generally live in marshes, shallow ponds, and slow-moving waterways, which accommodate their feeding habits.

The mallard is by far the most common of the dabbling ducks, quite possibly of all ducks. It is a common sight throughout the northern hemisphere, both in the wild and under domestication. When the word "duck" is mentioned, an image close to the typical mallard comes to mind for most people.

So widespread is the species that it has given rise to distinct populations, such as the geographically named Mexican duck and Mariana mallard. However, the latter is considered extinct, or nearly so, and the gene pool of the former has been so contaminated through the introduction of the primary mallard species that it is no longer considered its own full species.

The strength of the mallard's genetic make-up and its ability to adapt as it expands its range has served to the detriment of many other duck species. The black duck of North America, for example, has been in decline for decades and part of the reason is hybridization as a result of crossbreeding with mallards.

Mallards are extremely social birds, rarely found as single specimens, but rather almost always gathering in flocks, sometimes very large ones, in which they have no problems mixing with other duck species. Wild mallards are generally wary, but those that take up residence in parks quickly become tame enough for near contact with humans, eagerly rushing from one offering of free food to the next.

In nest site choices, the mallard continues its cosmopolitan nature. Nests are commonly hidden among vegetation on the ground, placed in tree cavities, and atop abandoned

FOLLOWING PAGE: Survival rates among young ducks, like these two-week-old mallards, is quite low. Many creatures prey on the fledglings, from snapping turtles to hawks.

The familiar mallard has been the original ancestor of many domestic waterfowl breeds now common and spread worldwide, but still exhibiting traits of the original parentage.

Although the mallard in the wild is normally a very shy bird, individuals and flocks that take up residence in locations close to humans, such as city parks, quickly become quite tame.

nests of other large birds. Distance of the nest from the nearest body of water generally does not appear to be a concern for the duck.

Sometimes considered a race of the mallard rather than its own distinct species is the mottled duck of the coastal southeastern United States. Although its range and that of the black duck overlaps very little, the mottled duck appears to be an intermediate species between the mallard and the black.

The mottled duck has an extremely long breeding season. Although the mating peak occurs in May and June, breeding may happen any time from February through August. The high rate of nest predation by a wide array of creatures on the mottled duck's nest, which

is on the ground hidden among vegetation, is among the reasons for the prolonged breeding period.

The aptly named American black duck is the darkest of the mallard group. Blackish-brown, pale brown, and dull buff are the colors of the species. The black duck is an abundant species, widespread across eastern North America, but it is suffering a very sharp decline. From an estimated four million birds in the 1950s, the population was reduced by about 40 percent less than ten years later. The decline has not stopped. Competition and hybridization with the mallard must be a factor, although the intricacies of the black duck's overall situation are not yet fully understood.

After mating, the male mallard joins other males of the species to molt, leaving the female to hatch out the eggs and tend to the young hatchlings.

The female mallard is highly protective of her young, although her principle means of defense is leading her brood away from whatever she perceives as a threat.

The muscovy duck, native to Central and South America, is another species of dabbling duck that has been widely introduced to regions outside its native range, primarily as a domestic fowl. The iridescent greenish-black of the wild birds has been replaced by a near rainbow of colors in the domestication process. The characteristic that has stayed with the species is the red knob at the base of the drake's bill surrounded by red skin.

In the wild state, the muscovy duck is one of those species that make nomadic flights for breeding when the savannas are flooded by seasonal rains. Much of the rest of the year is spent in the forest, where the birds roost in small flocks in trees and feed in mashes on leaves and seeds, as well as fish, crustaceans, herptiles, and insects. They also prefer to make their nests in tree cavities.

The male wood duck of the eastern United States and the mandarin of Asia are among the most colorful of the dabbling ducks. The male woodie is virtually a rainbow of color, from the iridescent green of its crested head to its ruddy breast to the patches of sky blue along its wings. The male Mandarin shows an oversized

The muscovy duck is widely known as a bulky domestic fowl, but the wild ancestor from which it was derived is a much sleeker bird of the tropical forest.

The first flight for wood duck nestlings is often a plummeting plunge to the water below their nest, which regularly is many feet up in a cavity inside a tree.

The common names of many waterfowl species are highly and accurately descriptive. The wood duck, for example, is a duck of the woodlands. It nests in cavities in trees, and feeds heavily on the fruits of woodland plants.

head area with orangish sails, white head band, and red bill, as well as a bright orange rump area. Both species generally place their nests in tree cavities, rather than on the ground.

The beautiful coloration of the male wood duck nearly led to the species' extinction in the nineteenth century, as market hunters pursued the birds to satisfy demand for its feathers for fashion decorations and to produce flies for fishing. Conservation measures were put in place in time to save the species, a cavity-nester, which also responded well to the

efforts by sportsmen to place wood duck nesting boxes in widespread waters. Today, the wood duck has recovered to the point that there is a sufficient population to permit sport hunting with no detriment to the species.

The mandarin is the familiar duck depicted in Chinese and Japanese art. It also has been an immensely popular species in the domestic fowl trade, which led to large-scale exportation in the past. The Chinese government banned exportation in 1975, but such exploitation, along with the wholesale destruction of its forested habitat, led to severe declines in the species' population. Today, there may be as many feral mandarins in Great Britain as in its native range, an estimated one thousand pairs in each region. The British feral population, composed of escapees from domestication and their descendants, is an important subset of the world's total population, estimated at no more than five thousand pairs.

The cotton pygmy goose, measuring no more than 14 inches (355 mm) in length, is the smallest of all wild fowl. It also is a very widespread species, ranging across tropical Asia and into northeastern Australia, which leads to a rather varied breeding season across its range. In Australia, for example, the breeding season is January through March, while

The male wood duck of North America is considered by many to be among the most beautiful of all ducks. Particularly in breeding season, the bird is unmistakable to even novice waterfowl enthusiasts.

As even the casual observer might guess, the Mandarin duck of Asia is closely related to the wood duck of North America. The former also rivals the latter as the most beautiful of the ducks.

in northern India it extends from June through September. It shows a decided preference for staying off dry land, spending most of its time on the water or on projecting stumps. It is an extremely buoyant swimmer, skimming the surface of the water for its food and sometimes diving. The Asian population is abundant, but the Australian race has been losing ground in the face of wetland draining.

Huge flocks of American wigeon are regularly spotted on the wintering grounds south to the Gulf of Mexico. They have been

documented in the tens of thousands. But, in spring, the flocks break up into pairs, which scatter northward into the prairie pothole and muskeg regions of North America.

The wigeon is grouped with the dabbling ducks, but a substantial amount of its food, particularly when gathered in large flocks, is obtained by grazing in fields, pastures, and marshlands.

Localized dips and recoveries in numbers aside, the gadwall remains an extremely widespread and abundant species across the northern hemisphere. It's North American population numbers in the millions, while the Eurasian population has been estimated in the hundreds of thousands and possibly on the rise. The male gadwall is not a particularly colorful bird, but its dark gray body, brownish head, and nearly black rump with no white marking at all is a distinctive, easily identifiable pattern.

The blue-winged, green-winged, and cinnamon teals are among the smallest of the dabbling ducks. While the mallard measures 25 inches (635mm) in length, the maximum lengths for the teals are 16 inches (406mm), 15 inches (380mm), and 19 inches (482mm) respectively. All three teal species are prized by hunters, both for their fast, agile, twisting, and

Unlike a great many species of ducks, the male of the Chiloe wigeon helps the female in tending their hatchlings.

turning flight that makes them a challenging target, and for their quality on the table.

The blue-winged teal is a highly migratory species, generally following inland routes rather than those along the coast. The species is the long-distance champion of the Americas, breeding in North America, but wintering as far south as Argentina. It rarely comes far onto land, but is at ease on shores, protruding stumps, and branches. Its nest is generally concealed in shoreline vegetation.

Green-winged teals can fly almost straight up into the air when surprised. This ability has produced a common description of a flock of these birds as a "spring of teal". In the air, the flock flies in a tight pattern, twisting, and turning in near perfect unison.

Five different races of cinnamon teal are recognized, although there have been no reported sightings of the borreroi race of Colombia for many years. The species is closely related to the blue-winged teal and shares many of the habits and behaviors.

The aptly named yellow-billed duck is the only wild duck in Africa with yellow on its bill. With that distinction it is unlikely that the yellow-billed duck would be confused with any other species in Africa, although the dark body colorings are close to that of the African black duck. Yellow-billed ducks are very social waterfowl, coming together in very large flocks during the dry season. Those flocks disperse quickly into breeding pairs with the arrival of rains. Birds may fly more than 625 miles (1,000 km) in search of suitable waters for breeding. Because the rains are the trigger for breeding activity and they are irregular, the breeding season for the yellow-billed duck can vary widely.

The green-winged teal is an acrobatic flyer, despite the awkward gait its short stubby legs give it on land.

The bill also provided the name for the spotbill of southern Asia, the males of which sport a mostly black bill that ends in a spot of bright yellow at the tip, and red at the base. Although the spotbill is a social bird that regularly flocks with other dabbling ducks, it rarely is found in groups of more than a few dozen. The spotbill population is composed of separate races in India and Burma, and a third race in China which lacks the red at the base of the bill.

Long-tail streamers arch out over the water as the drake northern pintail swims along. The four-inch (100 mm) streamers are the namesake for the species, which is found in large numbers in Eurasia and North America. The large population is regularly attracted by harvested grainfields which may draw as many as a half-million of these birds to a single site. In some areas, farmers plant fields to be left just for the pintails in attempts to draw the birds from other fields.

When harvested grainfields are not available, the pintail feeds on the water, where its relatively long neck allows it to reach deeper than other ducks in the same range. This trait permits the pintail to utilize additional areas of the various bodies of water, the bottoms of which are out of reach for the other species.

The South American counterpart to the northern pintail is the yellow-billed pintail, which occurs in three races across South America. The yellow sides to the bill, of course, lends the species its name. The yellow-billed pintail does not share the gregarious nature of its cousin to the north, and at times other than the breeding season is most often found in small flocks. It also is not attracted to grainfields, although it will supplement its aquatic diet with vegetation grazed from grasslands that occur next to water.

Red-billed teal, native to southern and eastern Africa, regularly form long-term mating bonds, and the drake often assists the hen in tending to the ducklings after they have hatched. In the non-breeding portions of the year, the sociable species often gathers in huge flocks. Numbers in those flocks have been estimated as high as 500,000, and the red-billed teal is considered the most abundant duck across its range. The red-billed teal is another of those duck species highly dependent on the seasonal nature of rainfall in much of Africa. Breeding almost always begins immediately after significant rains have come, and the largest concentrations have been documented at the ends of rainy seasons.

There are also huge numbers of garganey, a highly migratory species that breeds in Europe and central Asia and winters in sub-Saharan Africa. Immense flocks of tens of thousands of garganey, flying in a densely packed formation, are regularly seen flying low over the Black Sea and Mediterranean Sea. They often roost on the sea for much of the day before continuing on with their migration late in the afternoon.

As the northern shoveler swims along with the front half of its bill underwater, water flows through the bill and bits of food are screened from the water by projections from the top and bottom portions of the bill. The species' namesake bill is designed to be a portable filter for tiny seeds and aquatic animals that the shoveler eats. Although the northern shoveler will dabble for food, its preferred seining method of feeding provides a niche with little competition from other waterfowl species.

Flocks of northern shovelers are often seen swimming in slow circles repeatedly through the same area of a body of water. The action of their paddling stirs up the water and the bottom, freeing the seeds and animals to float to the surface.

The northern pintail is another very aptly named duck species. The namesake pintail feathering makes for easy identification.

The northern shoveler often feeds by swinging its broad bill back and forth across the surface of the water, sifting out edible morsels.

Pochards

The marbled duck of southern Europe and central Asia is another social species, usually seen in small flocks, even during the breeding season. When there are large numbers on a breeding ground, the birds will tolerate their nests to be in very close proximity, although under less numerous situations they will space them farther apart.

Popular with waterfowl breeders, the wild population of the red-crested pochard has been expanding its range north into France, the Netherlands, and Denmark over the past several decades. Much of the expansion has occurred naturally, but the actual size of this natural expansion is uncertain because of birds that have escaped from domestication mixing with the wild ones.

Males and immature birds of this largest of the pochard ducks regularly make extensive molt migrations, about the time the females are nearing the end of incubation on their eggs. Large numbers of the males and immatures can be found on large, deep, freshwater lakes at this time. Otherwise, the red-crested pochard is generally found in only small flocks on similar waters.

Canvasbacks regularly feed on aquatic vegetation brought up from the bottoms of ponds at depths down to 30 feet (9 meters). And often, when they return to the surface with their meal, they are chased by coots and wigeons attempting to steal it.

The population of this North American species has seen sharp rises and declines throughout recorded history, largely tied to conditions in the continent's prairie pothole region. When a series of severe droughts struck the region in the 1930s, breeding success and population numbers plummeted.

Although the Eurasian pochard is a social bird by day, regularly gathering in mixed flocks of many species, the groups of pochards within those larger flocks tend to move off by themselves to sleep. The species tends to be most active in the early morning and late evening, spending most daylight hours in large, densely packed rafts of birds on large bodies of water. Smaller groups can be found passing the day on shore as well.

The canvasback is among the fastest flying of the ducks, having been clocked at more than 70 miles (112km) per hour.

Males and non-paired red-crested pochards regularly make long molt migrations in mid-summer, moving considerable distances from their breeding grounds.

Widespread across North America, the red-head is a very social species during the non-breeding seasons. It regularly gathers in extremely large flocks with its own species and other similar species on coastal lagoons, tidal bays, and freshwater lakes, where it floats as part of the raft throughout much of the day. But after the drakes and hens have paired off in midwinter and moved to the breeding grounds, they tend to establish relatively large territories around their nests, which often are placed partly in the water. The hens also are known to regularly deposit their eggs in the nests of other waterbirds within their territories.

Although the redhead's population numbers have varied with the fortunes of its prairie pothole breeding grounds, it has stabilized in recent decades and even begun to spread eastward into the Great Lakes regions.

The common name of the ring-necked duck seems appropriate only under close examination. The dull ruddy neck ring of the drake is extremely difficult to spot at any distance. While it regularly gathers in flocks with other pochards, the ring-necked duck tends to feed in much shallower water than others of the group by diving, dabbling, and upending. And, while it shares the large-water preferences

As man drained many of the wetlands in the prairie region of North America, the redhead population declined drastically. It has responded to habitat restoration efforts.

of its fellows during the non-breeding seasons, when it comes to nesting the ring-necked duck often gravitates to very small marshland pools. Its nest is often placed on floating vegetation, small islands, and submerged stumps.

For a pochard, the ferruginous duck of eastern Europe and Asia tends to most often be found in very small groups. Only after the post-breeding molt, in preparation for migration, does the species gather in any numbers, and even then a few hundred ferruginous ducks are a large number to be gathered together.

Individually, the ferruginous duck also enjoys a good measure of solitude on the freshwater lakes and marshlands it inhabits.

The common name of the ring-necked is appropriate only under close inspection. The ring is dull and nearly impossible to spot in the wild.

Oil spills in important wintering areas have played a part in the drastic drop in population of the canvasback, which may have lost half of its entire species during the early 1970s.

FOLLOWING PAGE: *Although an entire flock of ducks may appear to be at rest or asleep, at least a few individuals are almost always alert and ready to warn their fellows of any potential threats.*

Animals make up a larger portion of the diet of some duck species than is generally assumed. About half of the diet of the greater scaup, for example, is animal matter.

It's a rather shy bird that tends to stay close to emergent water plants. When these factors are combined, the species offers a challenge to would-be counters, making accurate population numbers difficult.

The tufted duck, with its namesake tuft of feathers at the back of its head, is the most abundant of the pochards. It breeds throughout the Palaearctic regions of Europe and Asia, and it is believed that hundreds of thousands winter across the two continents. It's another highly social species and can be found in flocks throughout the year, although gatherings of considerable size occur only on the wintering grounds. Nests are often placed in close proximity to one another, as well as among the colonial nests of gulls.

The tufted duck is a premier diving bird. It can submerge to depths as great as 20 feet (6 meters) and can remain underwater for as long as 30 seconds in search of the mollusks and other aquatic life that form the basis of its diet.

Occurring transglobally in the northern hemisphere, the greater scaup is another social bird often found in flocks of various sizes at times other than the breeding season. However, on the wintering grounds those flocks tend to be sexually segregated. Drakes tend to spend the winter farther north than hens, and the sexually immature birds of the year tend to gather in flocks of their own, apart from either grouping of adults. The greater scaup is a marine species for much of the year, but moves to freshwater bodies to breed. It spends the winter on shallow coastal waters, feeding in rhythm with the tides.

Like its larger cousin, the lesser scaup is an abundant and widespread species. It is probably the most abundant waterfowl species of North America. Although it too is commonly found on coastal waters, the lesser scaup shows a decided preference for freshwater bodies. Huge flocks congregate on lowland lakes over the winter.

The lesser scaup is one of the most numerous and widely dispersed ducks species across North America.

Sea Ducks

As the group name implies, most members of the sea duck tribe are closely tied to coastal and estuary waters, but many also occur on freshwater lakes and along rivers.

Famed eider down is the down that the hen of the common eider plucks from her own breast to line the interior of her nest. Even in this day of incredibly efficient man-made materials, eider down continues to enjoy a well-earned reputation for insulation. Breeding colonies of as many as 10,000 of these ducks have been protected and enhanced in Iceland and Norway as a source of the down, which is collected, cleaned and sold to manufacturers of sleeping bags, down outerwear and quilts.

The insulation created in the common eider's nest by the downy lining allows the hen to incubate her four to six olive-green eggs for just four weeks before they hatch. The ducklings that emerge generally join with those from other broods in nurseries.

The king eider—the drake of which is one of the most beautiful waterfowl—is much more migratory than the common eider. Its breeding grounds on the tundra of the high Arctic are completely abandoned in winter,

Many species of ducks choose to breed along large, slow bodies of water. The harlequin duck, however, makes its nest along swiftly moving rivers.

when the birds congregate on open oceans and bays along the coast that remain ice free. At that time of year, when the bird is not diving for food, it rests on ice flows and on the shore.

Although the king eider is hunted heavily by native people in some parts of the Arctic, such activity appears to have little impact on the overall population. The species is generally considered one of the most abundant of waterfowl species.

The brilliantly colored harlequin duck of northern Europe, Asia, and North America is a highly skilled swimmer, at home in fast-flowing water. It is able to use rapids and currents to move upstream or down with nearly equal ease. It makes full use of eddies and slack water to half-fly, half-swim over the surface of the water. As it moves over the water, the harlequin twists and turns its body with every bend of the stream.

The common scoter is also known as the black scoter for its entirely black coloring, except for a yellow patch on its bill. The patch is larger in the North American race of the species than in the Eurasian race.

Courtship is a time of great activity for the common scoter, with males rushing at and chasing rival males in great sprays of water, and females also rushing at and fending off males they have rejected. The males indulge in a great deal of calling during this period, producing a musical whistle that sometimes can be heard hundreds of yards away.

Although the surf scoter is a native of North America, small numbers show up regularly in Great Britain, Japan, Siberia, and Hawaii. The bird is not common in those distant locales,

Breeding across most of the high-Arctic, the king eider is commonly observed resting on the edges of ice flows.

As with other colorations in many duck species, even the namesake eye of the common goldeneye is brighter and more vivid in the male of the species.

On the iridescent feathers of many brightly colored duck species, intensity of light and angle of light can cause a widely varied array of reflected coloring.

Most wild waterfowl have incredibly strong eyesight, which serves as their primary early warning system for dangers.

The common name of the bufflehead is derived from the words "buffalo head," which is how it was described by the first Europeans to observe the species.

but its huge bill with a brightly colored pattern enables ready and definitive identification. Such non-range visitors are known as vagrants, and the surf scoter is among the most frequent vagrants of North American waterfowl. The vagrant surf scoters that reach Europe regularly mix in with flocks of other scoter species.

The velvet or white-winged scoter is the largest of the scoters and is the only dark sea duck with white secondary feathers. These characteristics make for easy identification of a species that is widespread across the northern hemisphere. It's a very social bird, generally found in large flocks all year except for the breeding season, when it tends to be a solitary nester.

Diving Ducks

Diving ducks are so named because of their habit of diving to feed on water plants, fish, shellfish, and aquatic insects. Large lakes and seacoasts that provide abundant food are

their prime habitat. They generally spend their nights afloat on those waters, far from shore.

The oldsquaw is among the most accomplished of diving ducks, able to reach depths of 180 (55 meters) feet while staying underwater for as long as a minute in pursuit of fish, mollusks, and crustaceans.

The name of the bufflehead makes reference to the similarity of head shapes between the male of this species and the bull American bison or buffalo. The bufflehead is a small, restless duck, almost always on the move or involved in disputes with other ducks.

Mergansers, with their distinctive long, narrow, sawtooth-edged bills, are considered a separate subfamily from the other diving ducks. The mergasers are able anglers, and their fish-catching abilities have at times brought them into conflict with commercial and sport fishermen. However, their actual impact on a fishery is generally much lower than stated by their opponents.

A male red-breasted merganser proclaims his dominance over a selected nesting territory.

The male hooded merganser regularly raises the huge crest at the rear of its head into a showy fan when displaying for a potential mate.

Mergansers often gather in flocks throughout the year, although the greatest concentrations generally occur during the winter.

GEESE AND SWANS

Geese generally are much larger than ducks and have longer necks. The sexes, the male gander and the female goose, as well as immature birds all share similar colorings. Juvenile birds are known as goslings.

Like ducks, geese are found in most places across the face of the globe. The migrations of some species, such as North America's Canada goose, have gained a great deal of attention and acclaim.

Canada Geese

The Canada goose traditionally nests from the northern United States north to the Arctic tundra and winters as far south as Mexico. However, in recent decades, new populations of these birds have arisen south of the traditional breeding grounds. These new populations often do not migrate and are resident throughout the year.

Such resident populations, burgeoning in recent years, have become a problem for the agricultural community. While they rest overnight and during midday in protected spots, such as community parks, in the morning and again in the afternoon they invade farmers' fields to feed. Their large numbers and their year-round presence can have devastating impacts locally.

Although the Canada goose is a powerful flier, individuals show a decided affinity for the places where they were hatched, which has led to many distinctive races of the species.

The Canada goose, with a few other species like caribou and wildebeest, have come to symbolize the seasonal phenomenon known as migration across the globe.

The Canada goose also has come to symbolize a growing environmental problem for many states of the eastern and western United States, an overabundance of non-migratory flocks.

The Canada goose generally places its nest on dry ground near the edge of a body of water, lining the nest with down it plucks from its own body.

A Canada goose leads an exceptionally large brood of goslings across open water in Alaska.

Canada geese are consummate grazers, whether tipping to nip some greenery from the bottom of a pond or waddling through a farmer's field.

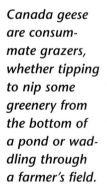

FOLLOWING PAGE: A family of geese cruises across the still waters of a Michigan lake during the brief dawn.

Snow Geese

Another species, the snow goose, continues its historic migrations but is becoming a problem species because of its increasimg numbers. Although farmers are reporting problems caused by wintering snow geese, the true area of concern is the species' breeding grounds in the far north. The birds, with the destructive habit of plucking an entire plant as they feed on aquatic vegetation, are literally eating themselves—and many other species—out of house and home.

Wildlife management agencies in Canada and the United States are taking extraordinary measures in attempts to deal with the approaching environmental disaster. These measures include liberal taking policies for native peoples in Canada, increasingly liberal seasons for hunters of the often hard-to-hunt birds and active nest-disturbance activities on the breeding grounds.

Domesticated Geese

Geese have been domesticated even longer than ducks. They are very hardy birds, providing products that at one time ranged from their abundant meat to their quills for use as writing instruments. Although quillpens today are a novelty, goose down is still highly prized for its softness in pillows and quilts, and for its insulating qualities in outerwear. Goose meat also is still sold commercially.

Geese also have been used on farms as guards for other domestic animals and birds because of their honking when predators and other threats approach, and for their aggressive nature when threatened.

Bean Geese

The bean goose is to northern Europe and Asia what the Canada goose is to North America. It breeds across that range in scattered pockets and is a very abundant species, increasing notably in some locales. The pink-foot goose, which winters primarily in Great Britain, often is considered a race of the bean goose rather than a species of its own.

A high-pitched call that sounds much like human laughter characterizes the white-fronted goose of northern Europe and Asia. The name for the bird in several European

Huge white clouds of snow geese move across sky and land in the Bosque del Apache National Wildlife Refuge in New Mexico.

The snow goose, with a swelling population and habitat-destroying style of feeding, is at the center of an environmental crisis in northern Canada.

Hawaiian goose, a species confined to the Hawaiian Islands and numbering more than 25,000 at the beginning of the twentieth century. By mid-century market hunting and introduced non-native predators had so badly decimated the population that the species was close to extinction. A captive breeding/wild release program has helped the species to recover to the point that it now numbers in the low thousands.

Barnacle Geese
Ancient Greelandish legend held that the goose barnacles found on the flotsam that drifts in the oceans of the north were actually the young of barnacle geese. It's pretty clear that the similarity of the coloring pattern of the bird's head and neck to the barnacle gave rise to the legend. In fact the goslings of the barnacle goose are produced on breeding grounds on Greenland and adjacent islands.

Brent Geese
The Brent goose is a very dark species of the high-Arctic tundra. Until the 1930s the bird's diet consisted mainly of eel-grass, which grows in dense beds in muddy estuaries of northwestern North America. But when a disease decimated the eel-grass, the Brent geese switched to grazing on pasturelands, developing a food preference that has continued to today.

Shelgeese
Shelducks and shelgeese are an intermediate group of birds between true ducks and true geese. The Egyptian goose of tropical Africa is one of these species. It's one of the most widespread of the waterfowl species in its range and is often abundant locally. The Egyptian goose is a capable swimmer and generally roosts on the water, but it also is seen regularly perching atop buildings, cliffs, and trees.

Ancient Norse legend held that goose barnacles floating amid flotsam in the ocean were actually baby barnacle geese.

languages translates into "laughing goose." It is an abundant and social species, regularly gathering in winter flocks of tens of thousands. As with many widespread species, there are several races; five in all, from *Anser albifrons albifrons* in Siberia to *Anser albifrons flavirostris* in Greenland.

Graylag Geese
The recent history of Eurasia's graylag goose has been one of ups and downs. The bird was once widespread across western Europe but went into drastic decline as marshlands were drained. In more recent times the species' numbers have climbed to the point that flocks of tens of thousands again can be observed and at times can cause damage to farmers' fields.

By 1952 there were only thirty remaining representatives of the highly terrestrial

The graylag goose, an abundant wild species across Europe and Asia, provided the wild ancestry for many of today's domestic breeds of geese.

The white-fronted goose, which breeds in the Siberian Arctic, is among the most shy species of geese. It prefers to keep distance between itself and all perceived threats.

The Cape Barren goose is an ancient Australian species, whose population has done remarkably well as man has brought large areas of Australia under cultivation.

The emperor goose is a fowl of the far north, breeding and wintering in Alaska and Siberia.

As with many species of geese, the Egyptian goose of Africa has thrived in locales where it has been introduced, such as Great Britain.

Swans

The tribe Cygnini—swans—is a distinctive, easily recognized group. Except for the black swan of Australia and New Zealand, and the black-necked swans of southern South America, all swan species are white (both sexes and immatures). Males are called cobs, females are called pens, and the young are called cygnets.

Without exception, all swans have extremely long necks and relatively small heads, which they submerge to feed. They also will upend to feed at greater depths, but they never dive unless injured or heavily pursued.

The swans are the largest of the waterfowl. The mute swan, for example, can measure more than five feet (1.5 meters) in length and weigh more than 30 pounds (13.5 kilograms).

Swans are noted for their grace on the water, although they take off rather heavily from the water's surface, generally pattering across the

Australia reluctantly opened a short hunting season to combat a population explosion of black swans in the wake of increased agricultural acreage.

The mute swan, an introduced resident of ponds and lakes in city parks and similar spots throughout the temperate world, has taken on a fairy-tale reputation for grace.

As with many native species of Australia, the black swan is a unique species among its closest relatives.

surface for considerable distances before rising. Once aloft, they are again quite graceful birds.

The mute swan, native to Eurasia but introduced in North America, Africa, and Australia, is the typical white swan of town parks. It is abundant, both in domestication and in the wild, and is noted for its aggressiveness. A pair of mute swans will put up a vigorous defense of the ground around the mound of vegetation that is their nest.

The flight call of the whooper swan is a deep "hoop-hoop," from which the Eurasian native garners its name. But the bird carries a wide repertoire of honks and trumpets, which it is constantly eager to bring into play. For example, every new arrival to a roosting flock on the water is greeted with a lasting chorus from the birds already gathered there.

The trumpeter swan of North America is another waterfowl species that came to the edge of extinction in the twentieth century. Market hunting for food, feathers, and down had reduced the birds to sixty-six individuals, all in Yellowstone National Park, by the 1930s. Conservation efforts, captive breeding, and relocation programs have made the trumpeter swan yet another of conservation's success stories. Their numbers today are estimated in the thousands.

Trumpeter swans, in their remarkable recovery from a few dozen birds in the 1930s to several thousand today, represents a true conservation success story.

A mute swan takes a nap in the typical waterfowl resting posture.

Flocks of tundra swans have been found to follow specific migration routes in their seasonal travels from breeding to wintering grounds.

Reintroduction efforts have brought the world population of trumpeter swans back to several thousand, more than two-thirds in Alaska.

Large flocks of mute swans have grown in many locales where just a few birds were introduced as domestic, ornamental species.

The trumpeter swan is at once the largest and least common of all swan species. Once abundant, the population was down to about 65 birds in Yellowstone National Park by the 1930s.

As a winter mist rises slowly, a flock of trumpeter swans emerges, resting on the ice.

Afterword

The family of waterfowl is a diverse group with representation, often in great numbers, across much of the earth. It is a family of great differences, from the tiny teal to the gigantic mute swan, from the colorful drake of the wood duck to the monotonous black of the common scoter.

It's a family of creatures to which humans have attached a history of traditions and practices. Hunters, domesticators, fanciers, birdwatchers—all have their connection to the world of waterfowl. Every school child knows that the passing of the great Vs of migration overhead signals the change of the seasons.

However, environmental changes can bring quick devastation. We've lost waterfowl species in the past. We have species on the brink of extinction right now. And, we most certainly will face the decline of others in the future, without the care and thought needed to keep the waterbirds of the world winging their way across the globe.

A pair of mute swans guards their nest, a huge mound of vegetation at lakeside, through a late snowfall in Germany.

INDEX

*Page numbers in **bold-face** type indicate photo captions.*